**Insight Text Guide**
Fiona Neilson

# Collected Stories

## Beverley Farmer

First published in 2007.

Insight Publications Pty Ltd
ABN 57 005 102 983
219 Glenhuntly Road,
Elsternwick Vic 3185
Australia.
Tel: +61 3 9523 0044
Fax: +61 3 9523 2044
Email: books@insightpublications.com.au

**www.insightpublications.com.au**

Cover Design: Graphic Partners
Internal Design & DTP: Sarn Potter
Editing: Robert Beardwood and Joanna Di Mattia
Printing: Print Impressions

National Library of Australia Cataloguing-in-Publication data:
Neilson, Fiona.
Beverley Farmer's Collected stories.
Bibliography.
For secondary school students.
ISBN 9781921088698 (pbk.).
1. Farmer, Beverley, 1941- Collected stories. I. Title.

A823.3

# contents

# CHARACTER TABLE

| Character | Stories | Description | Major relationship | Nature of relationship |
|---|---|---|---|---|
| **Marina** | 'Marina' | Newly married, young Greek-Australian woman. Suffers from depression. | Michali (husband) | Marriage is breaking down. |
| **Bell (child)** | 'The Harem' | Curious; does not fully understand the adult relationships around her. | Kate Peterson (neighbour) | Friends until they fall out over the crystal ball. |
| **Bell (adult)** | 'Place of Birth' & 'Pomegranates' | Australian woman. Pregnant in Greece, then revisits years later. Leaves her husband and son. | Grigori (husband) | Argue over where they should live. |
| | | | Kyria Sophia (mother-in-law) | Close, even after the divorce. |
| **Barbara** | 'Our Lady of the Beehives' & 'White Friday' | Australian woman who lives in Greece then Australia. Leaves her husband and sons. | Andoni (husband) | Argue over their roles within the family. |
| | | | Vassilaki (son) | Very close when he is little, then more distant as he grows older. |
| **Margaret** | 'Caffe Veneto' & 'Matrimonial Home' | Middle-aged woman whose husband leaves her. | Matthew (husband) | Attempt a reconciliation after his departure. |
| **Matthew** | | Middle-aged man who leaves his wife to have an affair. Unnamed in these stories. | Sandra (lover) | Travels with Sandra before deciding to return to his wife, Margaret. |
| **Anne** | | University student, daughter of Matthew and Margaret. | Matthew (father) | Seeks to show her father how much her mother will be hurt when he leaves her. |
| **Peter** | 'Fire and Flood' | Former teacher, now alcoholic after traumatic deaths. | Joan (partner) | A happy couple until Sam dies in a fire. Then a troubled relationship. |
| | | | Sam (Joan's son) | Like father and son; happy relationship. |
| | | | Marie (friend and lover) | Lovers after Joan's death. |

# INTRODUCTION

Beverley Farmer was born in Melbourne in 1941. In 1965 she married a Greek-Australian, moving to Greece in 1969 to live in a small farming village with her husband and his family. Like her characters Bell and Barbara, Farmer has lived between two different cultures. When she became pregnant, Farmer and her husband returned to Australia and she gave birth to a son in 1972. Despite their eventual divorce, Farmer has not severed her connection to Greece, returning many times to visit family and friends. Many of her short stories and novels, including an autobiographical work, are inspired by her overseas experiences. Farmer's first-hand experience of Greece and its people gives her stories with Greek settings a very strong sense of place.

Farmer's stories combine the horrific with the banal. They reveal ways in which ordinary lives can become involved in extraordinary events and chart the consequences of these encounters. Farmer presents the reader with a number of confronting and uncomfortable situations, including the adoption of a rapist narrator's point of view, the death of children and the ugly bullying of wives by their husbands.

At the same time, her stories are full of subtle observations about human relationships, such as the casual disdain that married couples can have towards one another and the doubts that people have about their ability to make sense of their lives. Placed amongst shocking tales are quieter, reflective stories about loneliness, motherhood, coming to terms with ageing and the connections between people on different sides of the world. Farmer explores the thoughts and feelings of very different people, from a traditional Greek grandmother to a young man on the brink of adulthood.

Farmer's language has been described as sensual, and these stories are full of evocative words and images. There is the grey blandness of life in Australian country towns in decades past, with flyblown meat and speckled apples. This is contrasted to the richness of village life in Greece, with syrupy pastries and freshly baked bread. Farmer takes her readers on an imaginative journey through a world of experiences, sights and tastes that leave a lingering impression of other lives and possibilities.

## A note on the text

The fourteen stories discussed in this guide were first published as a set in the collection *Home Time* (1985). Page numbers refer to the *Collected Stories* (UQP, 1996).

# BACKGROUND & CONTEXT

For Australian readers, many of Farmer's Australian stories are set in familiar surroundings: cities and regional towns, some by the beach and others in the country, with the familiar themes of bushfire, summer and school. Her Greek stories paint rich and vivid portraits of the towns and villages where they take place, creating a clear picture of them for readers who may not have travelled there. However, several areas of Greek culture, history and politics require further explanation if readers are to fully understand the stories that take place against these backdrops.

## Greek culture and tradition

Many of the Greek families that Farmer portrays are governed by a strong set of rules about proper roles and behaviour that may seem rigid when contrasted with contemporary Australian habits. These cultural differences are often illuminated by characters who challenge tradition. Bell and Barbara, for example, both leave their husbands and children in Greece and return to Australia. As foreigners or outsiders, Bell and Barbara highlight to the non-Greek reader some of the behaviour specific to the Greek way of life. Marriages and births are governed by practices and rituals that may seem perplexing to outsiders. It is important to understand that Greece is an old country where tradition, religion and superstition play a central role. Because of this history, it may be said that Greek people – especially those living in the towns and villages – have more rigid social roles than do people in a younger country like Australia.

Traditions related specifically to religious practices feature in Farmer's stories. The dominant religion in Greece is that of the Greek Orthodox Church, a form of Christianity. Both Marina in 'Marina' and Kyria Eirini in 'Our Lady of the Beehives' follow Greek Orthodox rituals such as lighting candles to the Panagia (Mary, mother of Jesus). Marina also has an icon or image of Christ and the Virgin Mary in her house, which she illuminates with a candle. She recalls the incense used during church ceremonies, which made her feel nauseous at her wedding because she was pregnant (p.21).

Religious ritual is closely linked to Greek folklore and superstition throughout Farmer's stories. Much of Kyria Eirini's behaviour, for example, is firmly linked to these beliefs. Linking religion and superstition, Kyria Eirini interprets the bee that stings Voula as a sign from the Panagia in response to her prayer. She and Marina also share a belief in the Evil Eye. This entails a belief that to be envious of another person, particularly of their good luck or good fortune, can bring about misfortune for that person. Marina has a shawl for her baby from her mother-in-law, with a blue bead on it to protect the baby from the Evil Eye (p.18). Kyria Eirini repeats a saying 'May we not cast the Evil Eye on her' (p.251) after praising Voula. These superstitions remain particularly strong amongst village women who maintain a more traditional way of life that has not been modernised in the way life in Greek cities has been.

## Greek history and political unrest

During World War II, Greece was invaded and occupied by Nazi forces from 1941–4. *Andartes* were armed bands that formed part of the Resistance movement against the occupying Germans and their allies, the Italians. The *andartes* controlled much of the countryside, but the Nazis subsequently carried out brutal retaliation, killing entire male populations of villages and displacing huge numbers of Greeks. Dimitroula in 'A Girl on the Sand' refers to her lover joining the *andartes*, and admits that she does not hold out hope of seeing him again. Dimitri recalls seeing many corpses during the German occupation (p.343).

After World War II, Greece found itself in the midst of a civil war that lasted from 1946–9. It was a war between Greek communists, including some of the groups that made up the Resistance movement, and the government's anti-communist armed forces. This war occurred at a time when governments in the West were concerned about communism taking control over large parts of Europe in the wake of World War II. When a ceasefire was declared in 1949, Greece's economy was in a dire state after so many years of war. Political upheaval continued in 1967, with a coup in which sections of the military overthrew the government on the grounds that it was too close to the Communist Party. A *junta,* or governing committee, was established and remained in power until 1974.

As a result of these political upheavals, many Greeks left their country in the early 1950s to settle in new places, one of which was Australia. The Australian government targeted Greeks (and Italians) through its immigration policy in the 1950s and 1960s, and Melbourne now has the largest population of Greeks outside of Greece itself. Stories such as 'Marina' and those involving Barbara and Bell show how migrants retain close ties with their families back in Greece and often return to visit them.

# GENRE, STRUCTURE & STYLE

## Genre

The texts in this collection are short stories of varying lengths that explore different characters' life experiences. They also convey a strong sense of the places and landscapes where the stories are set. Farmer's stories are contemporary Australian works of fiction that incorporate some of the author's personal history and experience. With a focus on people's personal journeys and interior lives, these stories are typically modern. While history does play a part in some of the stories, such as 'A Girl on the Sand', it is a backdrop that provides a context for the characters' behaviour rather than the point of the story itself.

Farmer's stories can also be described as belonging to the genre of realism. Realism does not seek to romanticise or cover up the sometimes gritty details about people's lives, but to present them as authentically as possible. Farmer does not gloss over Marina's postnatal depression or the domestic violence in 'Home Time'. She presents these as subjects worthy of literary attention and examines them in a daring way.

## Structure

An interesting feature of Farmer's stories is that a number of the characters and basic story-lines recur in at least one other story. For example, the story of the husband who leaves his wife and subsequently seeks reconciliation is told across two stories, 'Caffe Veneto' and 'Matrimonial Home'. In most of these pairings the second story takes place at a point in time later than the first story, with one exception: the order of 'Pomegranates' and 'Place of Birth' reverses the chronology. This collection presents the stories in the order in which they were written.

### Depicting the past

Within the actual stories, chronology is sometimes broken up and reordered, especially where a narrator recalls a past event. 'Fire and Flood' provides a strong example of this, where the narrator looks back to the events that have brought him to where he is today. This structure has the effect of stimulating the reader's curiosity: we know that a tragedy has occurred because we can see the aftermath, but we do not initially know what it is. The parts of 'Fire and Flood' that refer to the past help to explain those parts set in the present. 'A Girl on the Sand' also has a framing narrative set in the present, which contains the story from Dimitri's youth. Again, this flashback helps shape our understanding of who Dimitri is today.

### The act of writing

Another interesting structural feature is the prevalence of the act of writing within Farmer's stories. This is evident in 'A Man in the Laundrette', in which the young woman is in the process of writing the same story we are reading. In 'Home Time', the young woman writer has a conversation with another woman in a bar. Instead of relaying the conversation in dialogue, Farmer shows us the writing that the young woman produces after this conversation. Both stories tell us that this woman is a writer and point to the constructed nature of the texts that we are reading. Furthermore, they present the act of writing as a kind of refuge from the painful realities that they describe.

## Narrative points of view

'Our Lady of the Beehives' has a third-person omniscient narrator who enables the reader to access the thoughts of several different characters. The story employs this technique to offer readers a more comprehensive picture of the different threads of the story. Here the narrative point of view alternates between Barbara, Kyria Eirini and Voula. Through this style of narration we are able to see that while Eirini observes the flirtation between Voula and Andoni, Barbara is oblivious (unaware), preoccupied instead with her pregnancy and other thoughts.

Being able to share all three characters' thoughts and feelings also emphasises how all these people's lives are closely linked. In this way, it makes Andoni's potential infidelity even more morally dubious, as we are aware of the rifts that this would cause in the close family community surrounding him. In contrast, the two stories about the young woman writer and her boyfriend in the US, 'A Man in the Laundrette' and 'Home Time', only show us the thoughts of the young woman. We never learn what her boyfriend is thinking, which reinforces the sense of isolation that she is experiencing.

Only three of Farmer's stories have first-person narrators, and two of these place the reader in uncomfortable positions. 'A Woman with Black Hair' turns the reader into a voyeur as the rapist-narrator recounts his assault in graphic detail. We do not learn of the woman's experience directly from the narrative, although we can empathise. The rapist-narrator controls our view of the woman in the same way that he controls her. We are forced to share his first-hand account and may feel angry at this manipulation.

'Fire and Flood' also creates a sense of unease by bringing us close to Peter's pain and the awful events in his past. We share his terrible visions of Sam burning alive and relive the deterioration of his relationship with Joan as they both struggle to deal with this loss.

## Language

Farmer's language is rich and descriptive. It is also very literary, drawing on evocative images to create a sense of time and place. Read any sentence in her stories and look at how many adjectives are used. Farmer's language is not minimal or bare; rather, it is dense and poetic, and should be read slowly. Farmer also makes use of a variety of styles and voices in her stories. In 'The Harem' she uses a child's style of language, which is still descriptive but in a simpler register than some of the other stories.

Some of the stories, mainly the ones featuring an Australian protagonist in Greece, have untranslated Greek words and phrases. 'Our Lady of the Beehives', for example, replicates the types of conversations that go on in the story when English and Greek get mixed together. The use of Greek words conveys to a non-Greek reader the experience of being a foreigner, where certain objects and concepts remain mysterious because Farmer does not provide a translation.

# STORY-BY-STORY ANALYSIS

## 'Marina' (pp.18–26)

**Summary:** *Marina, a young Greek woman and migrant living in Melbourne, is at home with a newborn baby while her husband works in his pizza shop; she suspects him of having an affair; depressed and tired, unsure how to care for her new baby, Marina murders her child.*

This disturbing story is characterised from the start by its descriptions of the ugliness that Marina sees around her, such as her baby's blotchy skin, or her husband Michali's foul language (p.18). We wonder whether she is depressed and her reference to valium hints at this (p.19). Marina's reference to her baby as 'it' also does not sound like the loving attitude expected of mothers towards their children. Being a mother does not seem to come naturally to Marina; her experience of motherhood is painful and isolating. Her dream of her mother smashing the window in front of her (p.19) prefigures her act of violence towards her own child, just as her gruesome fantasies of the baby having accidents (pp.21, 23–4) anticipate its death.

The dramatic tension in the story builds as Marina's desperation mounts. Unable to contact her cherished mother-in-law in Greece, Marina goes to the beach for respite (a break), but this does not bring her any relief. We also wonder what Michali's reaction will be when he returns home, as he has expressed anger with Marina's inability to cope with the baby and does not try to understand what she is going through.

At the story's conclusion is a short scene that emphasises the ugliness of the baby's excrement and the pain of its nappy rash (pp.25–6). Pressure builds as the baby cries and Marina overturns a saucer of sour milk. In a moment of frustration and anger she murders her baby. The final image of Marina cradling her bloody, dead baby is grotesque and the reader is left to consider the true horror of the act.

***Q*** Do you feel empathy for Marina, or do you condemn her actions outright?

***Q*** How does Farmer suggest that Michali is also to blame for these events?

## 'The Harem' (pp.43–53)

**Summary:** *When Bell's father is transferred to a country town, she and her mother spend the school holidays with him; across the road lives a family where the husband, Mr Peterson, has a live-in lover, June Smith; Bell has a brief friendship with their daughter, Kate; when June and the family fall out, June moves in with Bell's family's landlord, Mr Grey.*

'The Harem' offers a view of adult sexuality through a child's perspective. Although the Petersons' family arrangement is highly unorthodox for the era and society in which the story is set, Bell does not remark on this. The adult reader pieces this together from comments made by other adults in the text. Bell calls the arrangement 'the Harem' without understanding what it means, and when she seeks clarification, her mother replies incorrectly that it is "Oh, a sort of Arab family" (p.44).

The non-monogamous sexual arrangement of the Peterson family is not the only aspect of these people that Bell's mother disapproves of. She would also prefer that Bell spent less time with them because they are of a lower social class. Bell instinctively realises that her mother disapproves and tells her that the Petersons gave her beer to drink so she will be banned from playing with Kate (p.50).

***Q*** In what way does the girls' quarrel over the glass egg mirror the adults' relationship?

## 'Caffe Veneto' (pp.191–203)

**Summary:** *Anne and her father meet for a meal at the Caffe Veneto, where he reveals an extramarital affair and his intentions to leave Anne's mother; Anne is shocked and explains that her mother would be devastated; a woman and her son sitting opposite overhear this conversation and the woman appears upset.*

**Note:** The father is only named as Matthew in 'Snowfall', one of the other stories in the collection. In 'Caffe Veneto' and 'Matrimonial Home' he is not referred to by name.

This story explores the ramifications of changing relationships and also a woman's realisation of the effect of men's behaviour. Farmer explores a daughter's growing understanding of her father as a man, with his own sexual desires and emotional life. Anne discovers that now she is an adult, she has to expand her role from that of daughter to confidante and advisor.

Anne's view of her parents as a unified part of her life is challenged. She is unsettled by the realisation that her father may break the family unit. At the same time, she feels complicit in her father's lies, because she already knows about previous infidelities. Although this is not the first time she has occupied the role of confidante, it is the first occasion where her mother's security is seriously threatened as a result.

The woman and her son who are also in the restaurant reinforce the theme of men who do wrong to women: the narrative implies that the woman is a mistress or ex-wife of a famous footballer (p.200). For Anne, this woman exemplifies the suffering of women who are ill-treated by men, and is an example of the pain her mother will suffer. She begins to see her father as the type of man who causes women pain. Anne asks her father not to leave her mother, and he reluctantly agrees.

***Q*** How do the different narrative points of view in this story illuminate the characters' feelings?

## 'Matrimonial Home' (pp.214–26)

***Summary:*** *Matthew has left his wife, Margaret; he visits her in his old home to see whether she will take him back after his affair with Sandra; they discuss what has happened and frankly explore their feelings; he stays the night in Margaret's bed, indicating a tentative reconciliation.*

Despite the fact that her husband has left her and turned her life upside down, Margaret manages to remain civil and generous when he calls to discuss their situation. It is a cathartic meeting because it enables both characters to express their feelings about past events. Margaret explains her shock when Matthew left her for another woman, while Matthew expresses disbelief at his own behaviour.

The story reveals the characters' desire to treat each other with consideration, despite Matthew's actions. He clearly feels guilty and does not expect his wife to accept him straight away, although he obviously hopes for a reconciliation, as does their daughter, Anne.

The characters' behaviour also illuminates the messiness of separation, where nothing is clear-cut or predictable. Instead of the separation being irrevocable and final, it is an uncertain process. The story shows the complexity of situations involving strong emotions and a long shared history between partners.

***Q*** How does the final paragraph suggest that Matthew will never change?

## 'Our Lady of the Beehives' (pp.237–58)

***Summary:*** *Barbara and Andoni are on holidays in Greece with their child Vassilaki and Andoni's mother, Kyria Eirini; Andoni and the landlord's teenage daughter Voula are attracted to each other; Eirini notices and prays to the Panagia to intervene; a bee stings Voula, triggering an accident in which Vassilaki is hurt, Andoni blames Voula; Eirini reads this as a sign from the Panagia.*

This story explores the threat posed to the dynamics of the family group by an outsider. It also examines Barbara's status, as a non-Greek woman who has married into a Greek family. It covers issues such as sexuality, the role of women and their reactions to men's infidelity, and the place of folklore or religious beliefs in the daily life of older Greek people.

The characters of Kyria Eirini, Voula and Barbara offer three different women's perspectives. Eirini understands what is happening between Voula and Andoni and realises, despairingly, that Andoni is following a similar pattern of behaviour to his deceased father, Vassili. Voula is also aware of the attraction between her and Andoni but she sees it from a limited perspective focused on her powers of seduction and not on the wider implications of her behaviour. Barbara's foreignness almost renders her meaningless in Voula's eyes: 'It was almost as if he were not married at all' (p.240). Barbara is focused on her pregnancy, which she announces to Andoni towards the end of the story, and also with experiencing the physical sensations of summer in Greece: the heat, sun and water.

***Q*** How do you interpret the bee incident: is it God's will or a random coincidence?

## 'A Man in the Laundrette' (pp.259–68)

***Summary:*** *A young woman writer is staying with her boyfriend in a US city; a young black man hassles her in the laundrette; her boyfriend twists the incident to imply that she led the man on and deserved it.*

This story is shaped by an underlying tension between the main character, the young woman writer; and her boyfriend, who is studying in the US. From the start she avoids disturbing him and relieves him of domestic tasks so he can focus on his work. Comments such as 'They were scrupulous about such matters when she first moved in' (p.259), and the reference to how he *used to* join her at the laundrette (p.263), show that the situation has changed. The boyfriend no longer contributes to their life in this way. The fact that he blames her for somehow attracting trouble reveals his feelings of resentment or distrust.

This story is also about the act of writing and who writes stories. In particular, it explores the difficulty women writers often find balancing writing with other demands on their time. The young woman subordinates (makes secondary) her writing to the needs of her boyfriend and to domestic tasks such as doing the laundry. While her boyfriend spends all day and many nights working undisturbed, she has to squeeze in her writing between all these other tasks. In the later story, 'Home Time', Farmer makes the problem of time and space explicit, indicating that the young woman's writing desk is 'also the table they eat at' (p.295).

This story questions whose version of the truth matters more. The young man sees his version of events in the laundrette as the correct one, despite not actually having witnessed what transpired. His interpretation of her story is unchallenged and is also supported by the Puerto Rican man, who helps the young woman but thinks she did not handle the situation correctly and is therefore to blame.

**KEY POINT**

Note that the woman is writing the same story as the one that we are reading.

***Q*** What do images of light and shade tell us about the state of this couple's relationship?

**Q** *"I had. It's finished."* What does the story's final line suggest about the future of their relationship?

## 'A Woman with Black Hair' (pp.269–75)

**Summary:** *A rapist stalks a woman who lives with her two young daughters, familiarising himself with her routines; one night he breaks into her house and rapes her.*

This story shocks with its graphic details of a sexual assault. From the start, several details alert the reader to the fact that the narrator poses a threat to the woman he describes. We wonder why he has observed her house and why he knows which of her doors lock. It soon becomes apparent, when he refers to his knife and his 'slit black tracksuit' (p.270), that he intends to harm her in both a physical and a sexual way. The reader's sense of unease grows as the man discloses more details about how he has watched her and left small signs that he has trespassed in her home.

**KEY POINT**

Images of cutting and slits in the rapist's description of the house carry violent sexual connotations.

While he is obsessed with the woman in the first half of the story, the rapist's attitude to her shifts after he has raped her. He is disgusted by her and thinks that 'She is nothing but a cringing sack of stained skin, this black-haired woman who for weeks has been an idol that I worshipped, my life's centre' (p.274). The story hints that his misogynistic attitude stems from once being mocked by a woman in the past and that these acts are his revenge (p.273). His speculation as to what she is thinking as she lies in her bed after the rape shows that he also wants to control her thoughts as part of his victimisation.

**Q** At what point do you become aware of the narrator's intentions? What narrative devices permit this understanding?

## 'Market Day' (pp.287–94)

**Summary:** *Mikri Elpida becomes aware of the fact that she is ageing when her niece, Nitsa, informs her that her hair is turning grey; Elpida regains her zest for life when Nitsa confides that she is in love with a student, Aleko.*

Elpida and Nitsa are sitting in a Greek village square on market day. Elpida revels in her memories and also in the sounds of the present, while Nitsa thinks about her boyfriend. Elpida feels old when young men approach their table and mistake her for Nitsa's grandmother, and when Nitsa tells her that her hair is now half grey. Elpida is shocked and reflects on her 'wasted life' (p.290).

In the evening Nitsa talks with her aunt to find out why she is sad. Although she does not refer to her sadness about ageing, Elpida confides that it is in part related to her blindness. Nitsa also confides that she feels sad about not being with her loved one, and asks Elpida to assist her in her love trysts. This shared confidence boosts Elpida's spirits and gives her renewed enthusiasm for life.

This story shows how the older generation may be revitalised through contact with the younger one. Elpida is genuinely excited at the "thrilling piece of news" (p.293) that Nitsa is in love, which seems to dull the pain of growing old. Elpida can live life vicariously through the eyes of a younger person who has her entire life ahead of her.

***Q*** Elpida is blind. What senses does she use to experience the world? How does the language of the story convey her sensations?

## 'Home Time' (pp.295–303)

**Summary:** *The same characters as in 'A Man in the Laundrette' visit a bar to watch* Casablanca*; afterwards the woman converses with an older woman who has been abused by her husband; when the couple return home, the man makes a violent gesture, spilling his coffee all over the woman's writing.*

As in 'A Man in the Laundrette', this story contains the narrative that the female character is writing. In this story, however, the excerpt is much longer and fills the reader in on what the two women discuss in the bar.

The older woman's story of the physical abuse she suffered at the hands of her husband, Andy, parallels the more subtle psychological abuse that the young woman writer is experiencing with her boyfriend.

The older woman's story shows the complex nature of a relationship between an abuser and their victim. Despite receiving horrible physical injuries, the woman nevertheless felt desolate when Andy left her, and she fondly recalls the start of their relationship. The abuse has, however, left her feeling cynical about relationships with men, describing the barbed comments that she and her second husband, Bill, aim at one another. She also comments on the younger woman's partner, noticing that 'Your man's been watching you all this time' (p.302) and how both men have 'suspicious eyes' (p.302) and lack trust.

**Key Point**

The classic romance film, *Casablanca*, provides an ironic juxtaposition to the lack of romance in the women's lives.

The Australian man's violent gesture of breaking the coffee cup and splattering the pages of the story shows that both the subject of the writing and the act of writing upset him. It is possible that he feels threatened by his girlfriend's writing. He does not want to feature in it as a character; perhaps he also feels competitive towards her and envies her talent. His anger manifests in this attack against both her and her work.

## 'White Friday' (pp.304–12)

**Summary:** *Barbara returns to Hydra, Greece, to see her sons, who live with her ex-husband; she is trying to decide whether to return to live in Greece or to stay in Australia, where she has an uncertain relationship with a man; she decides to go back to Australia.*

Years have passed since 'Our Lady of the Beehives' and Barbara is now divorced from her former husband, who is living in Greece with their two sons and a new wife. She has travelled to visit her children. The divorce is revealed through Barbara's conversation with an old woman she meets while walking, though no reason is given.

Barbara is at a turning point. She is unsure where her relationship with a new man is headed and she contemplates returning permanently to Greece, now that her mother is dead. Her mother's death has liberated her from the responsibility of staying in Australia and given her enough money to live in either country. Her mother's death has also focused Barbara's thoughts on mortality and how her two sons are her only remaining relatives.

**Key Point**

The story explores the theme of belonging and the idea that a shared history between people is not simply dissolved when they divorce.

Although Barbara is an Australian she has a strong attachment to the Greek landscape and village life. She feels at ease in traditional Greek culture and enjoys the physical sensations inspired by the sun and Greek food and wine. She feels torn between the future that the man in Australia may offer her, and a deep nostalgia for the life she once lived in Greece. Finally, Barbara decides to return, but the decision seems to make itself with little deliberation: 'Is this how decisions should be made or make themselves?' (p.312). Farmer also uses this story to suggest that people often make choices quickly based on their moods or a whim, rather than in a thoughtful or rational way.

***Q*** What does the conversation with the old woman cause Barbara to reflect on?

## 'Pomegranates' (pp.313–20)

**Summary:** *Bell visits a Greek village to see her former mother-in-law, who has aged noticeably since they last met; Bell remembers old times.*

Bell has left her Greek husband and their son and returned to Australia. While she is technically no longer part of the family she is warmly welcomed back by her former mother-in-law, Kyria Sophia, and the other villagers when she visits from Australia. Despite years of absence, Bell manages to enter into companionable activity with the women in her former husband's family. She helps them with the cooking and participates in other social activities such as taking tea with the seaman.

The story reveals Bell's earlier, difficult encounters with a foreign culture. We learn that her mother-in-law expected her to have children straight away and believed there was a medical problem when she did not. This expectation sits within the larger belief that God wills things to happen or not happen.

Sophia confronts the issue of Bell leaving her husband and son. She is not angry or aggressive, but expresses genuine regret at the way all their lives have turned out. At the same time, Bell's visit reminds Sophia of how she herself has aged, and she feels sad.

**KEY POINT**

Although 'Pomegranates' was written prior to 'Place of Birth', it recounts events that happen after those in the later story.

***Q*** "Where there's land, there's home" (p.316). What does 'Pomegranates' add to your understanding of the idea of 'home'?

## 'Fire and Flood' (pp.321–39)

**Summary:** *The narrator, Peter, is an alcoholic troubled by dreams where people die; he describes the death of his stepson in a bushfire, the deterioration of his relationship with the boy's mother, Joan, and her death in a flooded creek; after a brief relationship with Marie he leaves town.*

'Fire and Flood' presents the pain suffered in the aftermath of a child's death. The narrative conveys Peter and Joan's guilt and their recriminations against one another, as they wrestle with how to make sense of a senseless event. Both struggle with the realisation that neither of them was there when Sam died. The story builds up tension through disturbing images, such as the skinned snake turned inside out and the likening of the river's scum to vomit (p.323).

**KEY POINT**

Farmer's stories often demonstrate how our perceptions of the physical world are affected by our emotional state.

The story then compounds Peter's trauma when we learn that Joan has drowned in the flooded creek. Peter describes how he revisits the place where he used to live but has been forced to leave because people are suspicious of his involvement in two accidental deaths. Although he finds some comfort in an affair with Marie after Joan's death, the townspeople don't approve. Forced to leave his home, Peter lives an empty life in a city flat. The story does end on a note of hope, however, suggesting that through writing about the story, Peter may find a way of making sense of his experiences.

***Q*** Does the biblical allusion in the title 'Fire and Flood' suggest a wider meaning to be gained from the things that Peter suffers?

## 'A Girl on the Sand' (pp.340–56)

**Summary:** *Two stories intersect; a girl's body washes up on the sand in Australia, reminding Dimitri of a much earlier incident in his life in Greece when he met a young woman seeking an abortion and helped her.*

Dimitri or Jim is a Greek migrant who works in a restaurant by the coast. He receives a visit from his friend Jake, who has found a woman's dead body washed up on the shore. When Jake tells him that the woman is missing a hand, Dimitri remembers a girl he met in Thessaloniki when he was twelve years old, who also had a missing hand.

Dimitri met Dimitroula, a country girl, when she came to the bar where he worked wanting to know where she could obtain an abortion. He helped her while she was in town and, when she left, he fell in love with her. Even though he never sees her again, he looks out for her for many years. While the girl on the beach can't be Dimitroula, Dimitri feels there is a reason why he has been implicated (caught up) in this discovery.

In the background to this story is Dimitri's experience of World War II and the German occupation of Greece. It disrupted his family's life and forced him to face the death of many people. The story raises questions about how traditions and moral codes are changed by war and how social class may trap some people into a lifetime of poverty and misery.

***Q*** What does Dimitri mean when he refers to 'honour'? Do you think he behaves honourably?

## 'Place of Birth' (pp.357–78)

**Summary:** *Bell, who is pregnant, is staying with her husband Grigori at his parent's house in a Greek village over Christmas and New Year; her sister-in-law Chloe is also there with her two children; Bell decides to return to Australia to have their baby.*

Much of this story focuses on the dynamics between the family members, particularly between the women. Chloe, who is married to Grigori's brother, appears frustrated at having to stay with her in-laws while her husband is away, and she frequently complains. It also shows the hierarchy that exists in Greek society: as daughters-in-law, Bell and Chloe are expected to undertake household tasks and their father-in-law expresses disapproval when they don't. Bell also learns that it is her responsibility to intervene in family arguments as a representative of the family. However, Bell does not involve herself much in these family discussions, preferring instead to think about her pregnancy, and about the interesting photos that she can take.

Despite the fact that Bell comes from an Australian culture and the rest of the characters are Greek, they share many similarities and interact in the way that most families do when they spend time together. The story also shows how traditions from both families mix and mingle: for example, through their use of the Australian sixpence in the Christmas pudding.

Bell's overriding concern is where she will have her baby. A letter from her parents helps persuade her that it would be a good idea to return home, as they are getting old and infirm. However her husband Grigori is not impressed with her decision, telling her she is stubborn and thinks of no-one but herself (p.372). He feels that she has uprooted them too frequently.

***Q*** What is the significance of Bell's absence from many of the photos she takes?

# CHARACTERS & RELATIONSHIPS

## Marina

Key Quotes

'I'm afraid all the time.' (p.18)
'What can I do? Mamma, tell me.' (p.24)

Marina, the main character in 'Marina', is a depressed young Greek-Australian woman with a newborn baby. She lives in Melbourne with her Greek-Australian husband Michali and his daughter from a previous marriage, Eleni. We sense that she is suffering from postnatal depression, suggested by her lack of affection for her baby and her inability to see anything good around her. Marina also feels that her relationship with her husband has deteriorated and that he is repeating old patterns of infidelity, just as he did when they first met. She feels helpless and alone at home with her crying and vomiting baby. Her alienation is evident when she refers to the baby as 'it'.

Marina reaches out to her mother-in-law for help but cannot get through to her on the phone. She also seeks relief at the beach but the cold water stings her. In a moment of desperation she kills her baby. She feels relief as the baby is finally quiet.

Farmer indicates but does not explain that Marina has a problematic relationship with her own mother, Olga. She believes that her own mother hates her. However, Marina feels closer to Michali's mother, whom she affectionately calls 'Mamma'. She turns to Mamma in times of need, and writes to her to ask for help interpreting her dreams. Unfortunately, Marina is unable to contact Mamma and is abandoned when she needs someone to care for her most, with tragic consequences.

## Michali

Key Quote

'What the hell's wrong with you anyway, Rina?' (p.25)

Michali is a Greek-Australian pizza bar owner and Marina's husband. Marina and Michali had a good relationship during their courtship and early marriage that began to deteriorate prior to the baby's birth.

Michali chastises Marina for being unable to help him in his restaurant and crudely insults both her and the baby, yelling that their home is 'a madhouse and stank of shit.' (p.25). Marina suspects him of having an affair with Elly and finds him 'bestial' (p.25). He displays stereotypically sexist traits, including a lack of sensitivity towards Marina during this difficult time.

## Bell (child)

Key Quotes

"Mum, what's a harem?" (p.44)

'Her mother's answers were in such long words, Bell lost the thread, watching how the white bubbles heaved in a milkshake when you blew down the straw.' (p.52)

As a nine-year-old in 'The Harem', Bell witnesses some very adult events without realising what is going on. She is very observant and curious, and manages to pass on enough details so that we understand the true nature of what she is seeing and the relationships between the adults involved.

Bell plays with Kate, one of the few children her own age in the neighbourhood. She is mesmerised by Kate's glass egg and believes her when she says that she can read people's minds with it. When Kate becomes furious over Bell's attempt to see the egg again, Bell is upset. She inadvertently reveals to June that Kate has taken the egg, thereby triggering the event that brings June to Mr Grey.

## June Smith

Key Quote

'"Well, here I am, Tom Grey," she said. "If you still want me."' (p.52)

June Smith is a hairdresser in 'The Harem'. She has caused interest amongst the locals because she lives with Mr and Mrs Peterson and their daughter as Mr Peterson's mistress. It is this unconventional relationship which earns their home the nickname of the harem. She appears glamorous to Bell, with her dyed red hair and bubbly personality.

When June has an argument and leaves the Petersons, she comes straight to Tom Grey to ask if she can stay with him, which he agrees to.

As a single woman in 1950s or 1960s Australia, she uses her charm and attractiveness to men to survive.

## Barbara

Key Quotes

'Barbara came to life only in the sea. Her speckled body glowed, magnified ...' (p.243)

'She has been alone too long. The membranes that bind her to other lives have worn too thin to sustain her in motherhood.' (p.309)

Barbara (or 'Varvara') is an Australian woman married to a Greek man; her narrative is similar to that of the adult Bell. In 'Our Lady of the Beehives' she is pregnant with her second child. In 'White Friday', set many years later, she has divorced Andoni and returned to Australia, leaving him and their sons in Greece. On a trip back to Greece to see them she wonders whether to move back there to live. Her mother's recent death and questions about mortality are the impetus for Barbara's crisis, as she tries to decide where she belongs and the place to which she feels most strongly connected.

The narrative conveys Barbara's intense awareness of the physical sensations provided by her surroundings. In 'Our Lady of the Beehives' she is much more focused on herself and her pregnancy, and appears oblivious to the attraction that Voula holds for Andoni. In 'White Friday' she is less focused on place and more on relationships, in particular with the one she has with her lover back in Australia. Her frequent thoughts about this relationship play an important role in her decision to return home.

'White Friday' also shows Barbara's awareness that she has aged. The fragile nature of her relationship with her sons who live so far away makes her feel that she has lost something and will most likely never have any other children.

## Andoni Dimitriou

Key Quote

"It's your job to look after him. Why did you leave it to Voula?" (p.254)

Andoni is Barbara's husband in 'Our Lady of the Beehives' and then is her ex-husband in 'White Friday'. His character is not developed beyond a basic outline, and he serves more as the focus of Voula's interest than in any other role. His behaviour may be seen as selfish and sexist when he flirts with a teenage girl in front of his wife and family. He also blames Barbara for their son's accident even though she is not responsible for it.

## Kyria Eirini

Key Quote

'Pain is like salt, in a way, she thought; it can make the sweetness stronger, unless there's too much of it. Pain and sorrow and loss.' (p.258)

Kyria Eirini is Andoni's mother and keenly observes her son's attraction to Voula in 'Our Lady of the Beehives', praying that it will not develop any further. She is very religious and superstitious. Farmer shows this when Eirini goes to church to light a candle and pray that Barbara will become aware of her husband's potential infidelity and that Voula will be saved from temptation (p.244). When the bee sting incident turns Andoni against Voula, Eirini reads this as a sign that her prayer has been answered.

## Voula

Key Quote

'It was almost as if he were not married at all.' (p.240)

Voula is the teenage daughter of the Captain whose house Barbara and her family have rented for their seaside summer holiday. She has a romantic crush on Andoni and spends her time trying to find opportunities to flirt with him. When he takes the lead and flirts with her, however, she becomes uncomfortable and feels that the situation has gone too far (p.245). Voula is upset when she realises that Andoni blames her for Vassilaki's accident. Her experiences in the story represent a small coming of age, in which she has an unsettling but ultimately harmless encounter with adult sexuality.

## Bell (adult)

KEY QUOTES

'"Your hair's got darker," Kyria Sophia says, "since you came here first. Otherwise you're the same. Your Greek is still all right."' (p.313)

"I meant – I just feel – I want to go home and have it." (p.363)

Bell appears as a grown woman in 'Place of Birth', expecting her first child, and in 'Pomegranates', in which her son is older and she has been separated for a number of years from her husband, Grigori. Her life story is very similar to Barbara's.

KEY POINT

Although we assume that this is the same Bell as in 'The Harem', there are no meaningful or distinct links between that story and these to definitively confirm this.

In 'Place of Birth', Bell wants to return to Australia to have her baby because her parents are old. This causes conflict between her and Grigori, who feels as though he has to keep following her whenever she changes her mind about where to live. Bell is strongly driven by her instincts; her love of photography suggests a sensual relationship with the physical characteristics of a place which she tries to capture through her photos.

## Kyria Sophia

KEY QUOTE

"Can a woman just walk out on her man these days, and her little boy? Don't you remember how it was?" (p.320)

Kyria Sophia (Kyria means 'Mrs' in Greek) is Bell's mother-in-law and Grigori's mother; she appears in both 'Place of Birth' and 'Pomegranates.' She is Greek and lives in an unnamed Greek village. Hers is a simple, traditional lifestyle governed by the domestic routines of preparing meals, cleaning the house and looking after her grandchildren.

Kyria Sophia is superstitious, believing for example that the death of a baby during childbirth was a result of the mother's craving for fried bananas (p.359). We also find out in 'Pomegranates' that she previously interfered in Bell and Grigori's marriage because she was so keen for Bell to get pregnant (pp.316–7). When Bell revisits her many years later, Sophia greets her warmly, even though Bell has left her son and grandson. Although Sophia tries but fails to understand Bell's actions and motivation, she accepts her nonetheless. She reveals that she is sad about growing old at the very end of the story (p.320).

**Key Point**

Sophia and Bell's relationship is represented as a warm one despite the fact that Bell has left her husband and child. These characters' stories show that it is often impossible to separate a shared history.

## Grigori

**Key Quotes**

"You spring a thing like this on me. What I might feel – you couldn't care less, could you!" (p.363)

"You're a stubborn, selfish, cold-blooded woman, Bell. You always have been and you always will be." (p.372)

Grigori is Bell's husband. They visit his family in Greece when Bell is pregnant in 'Place of Birth'. He leaves the household chores to the women and spends time at the local cafe. He expects his Australian-born wife to assume her place in the family hierarchy, and does not defend her when Sophia interferes in their marriage.

Grigori is frustrated when Bell decides she wants to return to Australia to have their child. He believes that Bell gives too little consideration to what he wants, and prevents them from leading a settled life. He also accuses her of being selfish. In 'Pomegranates' we learn that Bell has left Grigori and their son, although we do not know the specific reasons why.

## Anne

**Key Quotes**

"I *fear* for my mother! … I fear for her! How will she bear it?" (p.198)

"You can choose not to know you're doing it, but still the damage is done. People suffer. Lives are ruined." (pp.200–1)

'She has a shrouded look, he thinks; her eyes, when for a moment she glances up, seem full of sorrow and foreboding.' (p.202)

Anne is Margaret and Matthew's daughter. In 'Caffe Veneto' she is a university student who is upset to learn that her father may leave her mother for a younger woman. In 'Matrimonial Home' she is hopeful that they will get back together again. Although she knows that her father has had affairs in the past, she is distressed in 'Caffe Veneto' when she finds that he intends to leave her mother this time. She spends most of the meal defending her mother's position and probable response to this news.

Anne is also sensitive to the feelings of the woman sitting nearby, whom she feels her father has upset (p.200). In many ways, Anne appears more mature and sensitive to the needs of others than her father is. Her own attitude to men and love seems to be shaped by her experience of her father's philandering.

## Margaret

Key Quote

"You had sentenced me to despair. I was left wondering how to live through even one day of it." (p.219)

Margaret is married to Matthew, with whom she has a daughter, Anne. She is the subject of their conversation in 'Caffe Veneto' but we do not meet her until 'Matrimonial Home.' The latter story is set some time after the end of the affair which is referred to in the earlier story. We hear about Margaret's despair when she returned from seeing her husband with his lover in Paris. She explains that she wondered how she could continue living, as this was the first time he had actually left her after numerous infidelities. When Matthew returns she accepts him. They attempt to reconcile, although she continues to wonder whether he will leave her again. Her doubts are evident as she cries when they go to bed together.

## Matthew

Key Quote

'His eyes are smaller ... This austerity of age, in his of all faces, is at the same time intimidating and pitiable. She wonders if he has seen it himself in mirrors.' (p.191)

KEY QUOTE

"In a sense you are the past, of course. You're the future as well. The only future that makes sense. At present, I'm stranded." (p.220)

*Note: This character is only named in 'Snowfall', one of the other stories in the collection. In 'Caffe Veneto' and 'Matrimonial Home' he is not referred to by name.*

Matthew is Anne's father and Margaret's philandering husband. He is a university lecturer who has fallen in love with one of his students, Sandra. We learn this in 'Caffe Veneto'. Here we see Matthew primarily through Anne's eyes and she sees him as an ageing middle-aged man desperately trying to hold onto his youth. He and Anne have a close relationship. He has told her about previous affairs and hopes that she will sympathise and support him again and not tell her mother.

Matthew seems incapable of comprehending the pain he will cause Margaret if he leaves her. In 'Caffe Veneto' he is sure that Margaret will find someone else, and does not seem to understand that this is not Anne's point. He tries to convince Anne to agree with his plan but she does not, and this flummoxes (confuses) him.

When Matthew visits Margaret in 'Matrimonial Home', he is conciliatory and listens as she explains her feelings. At the same time he wants a chance to explain himself. It is hard to tell whether he feels any remorse for the pain he has caused. On several occasions Margaret reminds him that: "I'm not the judge. I was the victim" (p.219). When she implores him to "Listen to me. You haven't been listening" (p.219), she indicates that she feels he hasn't really understood her perspective.

## Young woman

KEY QUOTES

"Loving someone's no *use*. And you only find out the hard way." (p.302)

'This time she knows better than to move until his footsteps creak away across the boards.' (p.303)

The young woman protagonist in 'A Man in the Laundrette' and 'Home Time' is an Australian visiting her boyfriend who is studying in the US. She spends her time writing. She is not named.

There is a distinct tension in her relationship with her boyfriend which is only made explicit at the end of 'Home Time', although it is evident in the earlier 'A Man in the Laundrette' from the start. The woman explains that she 'never wants to disturb him but she has to sometimes' (p.259). Farmer shows how she accommodates her boyfriend's study by making concessions to her own writing schedule, as if his needs are more important.

When her boyfriend interprets the incident in the laundrette as an example of her leading the other man on, the young woman is understandably shocked. He tells her that "Whenever you talk to a man, it's there" (p.267), which conflicts with her own experience of the incident, in which she felt like a victim of the black man's approaches.

'Home Time' develops these problems by exploring the young woman's continuing efforts to accommodate her boyfriend's needs. The final section of this story exposes his mistrust and jealousy towards her writing talent, and the violence that this engenders (causes).

## Young man

**Key quotes**

'He could be a statue or the shadow of one, a hard edge to the lamplight. He gives no sign of having heard.' (p.268)

"I am not to figure in anything you write ... Never." (p.303)

The young man in 'A Man in the Laundrette' and 'Home Time' is in the US writing a PhD thesis. His Australian girlfriend is living with him. He often disparages (criticises) and ignores her. When he reads what she has written after their evening out in the bar watching *Casablanca*, he becomes violent – not hitting her but spilling coffee all over her writing, showing complete disregard and contempt for what she has created and who she is.

Although we don't have access to his thoughts, the young man can be judged according to how he behaves towards his girlfriend. While she is concerned with making life as easy as possible for him, he seems motivated to antagonise (provoke) her because of jealousy towards her writing. The violent act that ends 'Home Time' leaves the reader concerned about how things may develop between them and whether he will become increasingly brutish and cruel.

## The rapist

**Key Quote**

> 'She is nothing but a cringing sack of stained skin, this black-haired woman who for weeks has been an idol that I worshipped, my life's centre.' (p.274)

The rapist in 'A Woman with Black Hair' is a meticulous planner who organises every aspect of his sexual assault and gains satisfaction from terrorising his victim. This is not the first assault he has carried out: his reference to how he has 'made a study of how to lose myself in these hushed suburban mornings' (p.275) shows his familiarity with escape routes. Statements such as 'None of these women' (p.273) clearly tell us that he has raped before.

The rapist has a misogynistic attitude towards women which surfaces once he has raped them. Farmer has the rapist describe the woman's beauty, her skin 'the colour of warm milk with honey' (p.269) and how he has 'chosen' her as his victim (p.271). He then shifts to despising her once he has raped her – he is disgusted by her 'slobber' and calls her a 'foul slut' (p.274). He is not aware how dangerously twisted the logic is of criticising a woman whom he has just raped for being sexually promiscuous.

One of the more disturbing aspects of this story is our inability to understand the rapist's motivation. He does hint that he has been sexually belittled in the past by a woman who had said, 'Mind if I go back to sleep now?' after sex (p.273). This may be one of the reasons why he tries to regain control through violence, asserting himself in the most heinous way over women. In contrast, he is able to observe and describe the woman's life and convey to readers a sense of the warmth and richness that exists there. By the story's conclusion, however, he remains completely untouched by this, hoping only to shatter the sanctity of her home.

## Mikri Elpida & Nitsa

**Key Quotes**

'What would Elpida know about love, though?' (p.288)
'She was a grey *yiayia*, she who had hardly lived.' (p.289)

The reader assumes that Mikri Elpida from 'Market Day' is middle-aged because she is disturbed to discover the first signs of ageing. For a long time she has been unaware of the changes in her physical appearance, mainly due to her blindness. Apparently none of the people around her has referred to these changes either. When Mikri Elpida spends time with her teenage niece, Nitsa, she becomes aware of the loss of her youth, which Farmer explores by contrasting the two women.

Nitsa has fallen in love with a student, Aleko, and spends her summer days thinking about him and ways that they can meet up. With the arrogance and innocence of youth, Nitsa seeks Elpida's advice about love but does not think that she knows anything about it.

Nitsa is initially unaware that she has hurt Elpida's feelings, but she later shows concern for her aunt. Nitsa's revelation that she has a boyfriend lifts Elpida's spirits, reconnecting her with the excitement of youth and of life generally.

## Peter

**Key Quotes**

'For the time being I need to live alone inside a web of black branches.' (p.321)
'A tower of strength. To think that she was looking to me for strength.' (p.335)

Peter is a former teacher and the narrator of 'Fire and Flood'. He loses first his stepson Sam and then his partner Joan in separate tragic accidents. When he recounts the story he is an alcoholic whose life has 'come to a standstill' (p.321). He needs to spend time alone to come to terms with what has happened, and he is still plagued by vivid dreams about the deaths. Peter finds it hard to distinguish the past from the present, a confusion that is evident when he corrects himself for phrases such as, 'Marie was – is – a teacher at the school' (p.328).

After Sam's death, Peter and Joan struggle to come to terms with the event and their relationship slowly breaks down. After Joan's death, Peter finds himself excluded from the town by people's suspicions and so leaves. When he visits the graves he feels that 'there was nowhere he wanted to live but in this town' (p.331). Peter has lost everything and struggles to understand what has happened and what his role in it was. He concludes that he has been used as the instrument of a kind of higher power (p.338), which the title 'Fire and Flood' also alludes to with its Biblical connotations. The final sentence suggests that he has recounted this story as a way of coming to terms with the past.

## Joan

**Key Quote**

"I can't stand it. That's all. I can only take so much. You just have to leave me alone." (p.330)

Joan is Peter's partner and Sam's mother in 'Fire and Flood'. She is a painter who expresses her feelings about her son's death by sketching burnt animals. Joan runs away from talking about Sam's death. She drowns when she falls into a flooded creek and is trapped by a tree.

## Dimitri

**Key Quote**

'Now our lives have crossed a second time – no, drawn close without touching, a second time. Lives with their roots not spread but sunk deep.' (p.355)

Dimitri, the narrator in 'A Girl on the Sand', is a Greek man living in Australia. He is nearly forty and works in a restaurant or cafe but is seeking to better himself by studying to become a teacher. His family emigrated fifteen years before the time of the story and has relaxed some of its traditional ways, although his mother is still hoping he will remarry.

Dimitri reflects on the hardships that his family and many Greek people endured during the wars and also through the harsh Greek climate. He has a strong sense of how his background and upbringing have shaped him. He appears happy with his current life, which is not as difficult as it once was.

Dimitri recalls the manner in which Dimitroula arrived at the bar. He had been kind to her even though he was not in a very secure situation himself. He fell in love with her and continued to carry a romantic ideal of her in his mind for years afterwards. After Jake tells him about the body on the beach Dimitri connects the dead girl to his lost love, and returns to the beach to contemplate the nature of this memory that has enabled him to reconnect with his past.

# THEMES, IDEAS & VALUES

## Cultural differences

KEY QUOTES

'"I might write letters home instead." Home is Australia. It's summer there.' (p.295)

'May your soil be barren so you don't have room to spread roots and so you keep groping deep.' (p.340)

Migrants and travellers feature in many of Farmer's stories, and their experiences not only tell us about cultural differences between Greece and Australia, but also reveal many universal aspects of human experience.

The Greek stories, such as 'Place of Birth' and 'Our Lady of the Beehives', explore traditional family structures and social roles through the eyes of the Australian female protagonists, Bell and Barbara. They convey the specific flavour of being an outsider in another culture through the use of Greek language, and through their foreigners' descriptions of customs and habits that are unknown in Western culture.

Conversely, a story such as 'A Girl on the Sand' shows the experience of Greek people who migrate to Australia. Dimitri explains how the customs of his Greek upbringing have slowly fallen by the wayside, such as the tradition for the son to marry before the younger sisters. Yet there are also physical and geographical similarities between the two countries, such as their interior barrenness.

## Female identity

Farmer's female characters often find themselves trapped between society's expectations on the one hand and biology on the other. Being a woman is presented as a curse in some of these stories. Characters such as Marina, Barbara and Bell feel trapped by their roles as wives and mothers. To escape this they find they must take drastic measures. The woman writer in 'Home Time' and 'A Man in the Laundrette' also seems trapped in a subservient role to her partner, and is blamed for a man's bad behaviour towards her.

Farmer explores the intersections between feminine identity, social expectations and motherhood. In 'A Woman with Black Hair', the reader is uncomfortably reminded that the rape victim is not only a woman but also a mother, whose children risk being drawn into the sphere of horror that the rapist sets up. Marina's problems centre on her inability to cope alone with her new baby. The adult Bell and Barbara characters in 'Pomegranates' and 'White Friday' are forced to reassess their role as mothers when both decide not to continue living with their children. The older women characters such as Kyria Sophia show how their role as mothers has been much less open to negotiation, which contrasts with the relative flexibility that both Barbara and Bell have been able to enjoy.

In Farmer's stories, female identity is often characterised by feelings of loss, alienation and estrangement. The woman writer in 'A Man in the Laundrette' and 'Home Time' embodies these feelings in two ways – she is living in a foreign country and her relationship lacks genuine warmth and intimacy. 'White Friday' and 'Pomegranates' show women who have separated from their closest relatives – their husbands and their children – but who return to the places and people of their past. In a way, their return serves as a melancholy reminder of what they have left behind.

## Male identity

Men are also important figures in Farmer's stories, sometimes in their own right, but often in contrast to lead female characters. Male behaviour varies throughout these stories. Some sexist behaviour occurs from Matthew in 'Matrimonial Home' and 'Caffe Veneto' when he seems unable to understand the ramifications of his behaviour for his wife. Like the actions of the young man in 'A Man in the Laundrette' and 'Home Time,' Matthew's behaviour can be seen as selfish and insensitive. Relations between men and women in Farmer's stories are often fraught with these problems.

However, there are more complex portraits of men in Farmer's stories. Although he is only casually drawn, Grigori in 'Place of Birth' is not a caricatured macho husband. Rather, he is a man concerned by the changes in his wife's mood and who expresses dismay that she wants to transplant their family yet again to return to Australia. This portrait shows that men are also the victims of women's decisions, and that a black-and-white reading of Farmer's stories that only considers female points of view is not possible.

## Family expectations

Key Quote

> "If she fights with her own mother it's her business. If she fights with mine it's my business and yours and all the family's." (p.371)

The Greek stories show the expectations placed upon family members to maintain the hierarchies that exist within traditional family structures. 'Place of Birth' shows Grigori becoming annoyed with Bell for not taking her mother-in-law's side in an argument with her sister-in-law. Yet while these hierarchies may seem rigid, they are open to renegotiation. The fact that both Bell and Barbara can return to their ex-in-laws after divorcing their Greek husbands shows the tolerance of their former close relatives, and illustrates that they are not rigidly stuck in tradition.

## Violence

Domestic violence and random acts of violence are a prominent feature of Farmer's stories, usually in the context of men being violent towards women. In 'A Girl on the Beach', the woman who is washed up is presumed to be the victim of a murder. The incident triggers a memory of the pregnancy and abortion of Dimitroula, who runs the risk of being assaulted by her aunt if she does not abort her baby. In 'Home Time', the older woman's account of the abuse she has suffered at the hands of her husband is paralleled by the emotional and psychological abuse that the young woman writer experiences in her relationship.

## Affairs and other illicit relationships

**Key Quotes**

"Yes, in an ideal world, people would all be faithful and all be secure. I agree. Or there'd be no love and so no insecurity." (p.195)

"It was the marriage you didn't want the last time I saw you. Now it's the divorce. No pleasing you, is there." (p.215)

Extramarital affairs run through many Farmer's stories. They reveal the difficulties often faced by married couples, exposing the dark underside to marriage and stability. Andoni is on the brink of seducing the teenage Voula in 'Our Lady of the Beehives', and the husband in 'Caffe Veneto' is contemplating an affair with one of his students, which we subsequently discover in 'Matrimonial Home' he has undertaken. 'The Harem' and 'Marina' also feature illicit relationships which have disruptive effects. In all cases, these relationships threaten the established order of family and couple relationships.

The themes of trust and betrayal serve to highlight how characters' expectations have been disappointed or frustrated, and explore the consequences of these betrayals. Marina feels betrayed when she suspects her husband of having an affair with Elly, and her despondency is at least in part a result of these suspicions. The husband in 'Caffe Veneto' betrays the trust of his wife and also of his daughter, to whom he has promised not to cheat on his wife. 'The Harem' points to the complex issues of trust and suspicion between the father-figure, Mr Peterson, and his rivals for affection, his daughter Kate and lover June.

## Loss, depression and despair

**Key Quotes**

'I might have been strong enough for her, but for my own sorrow. As it was, we both started drinking heavily, apart and together: red wine for preference, in those days. Drunk, we could communicate or at least fight openly.' (p.330)

'We are set in motion by a malevolent hand, unable to know in what our actions are rooted or what fruit they will bear. Why are we?' (p.338)

Just as many of Farmer's female characters convey a sense of loss because of the direction in which life has taken them, others display signs of depression and, more subtly, despair. Barbara in 'White Friday' alludes to this when she suggests that she is now so far removed from her sons' everyday lives that the only way that they will hear of her death will be in a telegram from the Australian Embassy. The story does not hint at any closeness or shared life between Barbara and her sons, and Barbara appears to be feeling the loss of these experiences and emotional bonds. In a more extreme example, Marina is obviously suffering from postnatal depression when she kills her baby.

'Fire and Flood' presents another extreme example of the alienation that can develop from despair. Peter feels alienated from his entire community, losing not only his loved ones but also his right to remain in the only place where he feels comfortable. When we meet him, he is living a rootless existence in the city, cut off from all that is meaningful to him.

'A Girl on the Sand', as well as chronicling the story of a Greek migrant family against a historical backdrop of the civil war, also depicts the personal cost of war through the loss of innocence experienced by both Dimitri and Dimitroula. Dimitri is only young when he encounters the pregnant Dimitroula, and he loses something of his childlike innocence through his exposure to Dimitroula's story. He learns about the precariousness of existence when one is a crippled woman, no matter how pretty, and about the desperation of people who have nothing to lose.

## Death

Farmer offers a range of perspectives on death, from violent and tragic deaths to an exploration of how ageing inexorably leads to it (see Ageing below). Death also prompts some of the characters to reflect on the nature of life and how they are living theirs.

The rapist in 'A Woman with Black Hair' uses the threat of death to force the woman not to resist his assault and to make her act out the scenario he has prepared for her. To make his threat serious, he cuts her skin so that she bleeds over her chest and hair. In 'Fire and Flood', characters succumb to violent but accidental deaths through being in the wrong place at the wrong time. The deaths of Sam and Joan have a far-reaching impact on Peter and also on members of the community, as they struggle to come to terms with the loss. Peter in particular is frozen in grief, unable to re-engage with life and incapable of making sense of what seem to be two cruelly random events. A larger concern of this story is how people attempt to understand traumatic events, and whether it is ever possible to find an explanation that encompasses such events.

The discovery of a dead girl in 'A Girl on the Beach' sets into motion Dimitri's recollections of an event that is in the distant past, and which also causes him to reflect on how his life has changed from its initial phase in Greece. For him, this death of a stranger does not bring about any closure; it does the opposite, raising more questions about the past. Death in this story does not simply cause melancholy reflection, but evokes many positive thoughts about the past.

## Ageing

**Key Quote**

'Bebeka means baby girl. Barbara is sorry not to have had a girl ... In a sense it's not too late; and yet it is. She has been alone too long.' (p.309)

'White Friday' makes explicit the link between growing old and dying. The mood of the story is a melancholy one, generated partly by Barbara's thoughts and also through her dream of death, her references to her mother's death and her observation of the sick cat on the pavement. The ashes created by the fire also allude to death and cremation, the inevitable culmination of the process of growing old. Barbara's thought that she may never have another child is also a sign of her ageing, as it signifies that the childbearing phase of her life is drawing to a close.

'Market Day' also deals with ageing and death: although the visit to the old aunt in hospital is brief, it casts a sombre shadow over the story and both Nitsa and Mikri Elpida think about it afterwards. The main focus of the story is on Mikri Elpida's sudden and unpleasant realisation that she is growing old and that her youthfulness, symbolised by her now greying bronze hair, is slipping away. Similarly, hair colour is used as a sign of ageing in 'Pomegranates', when Kyria Sophia asks Bell whether her hair is much whiter than when she last visited. This story ends on a melancholy tone as both Bell and Sophia realise that although they have been able to pick up the threads of their common past life, time has passed and things have changed, and the past remains in the past.

## Literary vocation

Key Quote

'It was not what she had meant to write, but it would have to do ... A couple of pages, that was all, in two years. She was always tired.' (p.238)

Like the creator of these stories, many of the female characters have chosen an artistic vocation. Many write stories or poems or take photographs, and it is worth considering the significance of this minor theme. Farmer's stories suggest that it is often difficult for women to balance their desire to write or create with their responsibilities to children, family and loved ones.

Barbara in 'White Friday' notes down diary entries and short poems; she also used to write reflective observations of her baby, as shown in 'Our Lady of the Beehives'. These notes serve to share with the reader some of her more intimate thoughts, and in 'Our Lady of the Beehives' we also see how having a baby has seriously curtailed her writing endeavours, as she has only written a couple of pages in two years. The older Barbara appears to have more time to write, now that she is on her own. Bell in 'Place of Birth' photographs her family and other people in the Greek village, as though she is recording something that she will not return to.

The woman writer in 'A Man in the Laundrette' and 'Home Time' works on incorporating her lived experience into her writing. While her experience in the laundrette and her boyfriend's response to it are disturbing, the woman is able to regain control and make sense of these events by writing about them. Writing is represented as a way of making sense of one's life and also potentially re-creating it. The reader knows that the relationship between the writer and her partner is deteriorating, which his reaction to the laundrette incident makes clear. Isolated in a foreign, unfriendly land with a non-committal partner, the woman writer is at least able to create something that is uniquely hers, and which allows her to express her feelings and reactions.

## Tradition and religion

In the Greek stories, some characters' beliefs in religion and tradition shape their behaviour. Kyria Sophia in 'Our Lady of the Beehives' provides a clear example through her praying to the Panagia (the Madonna, or Mary, mother of Jesus). She prays for Andoni not to be tempted by Voula, and for Barbara to become aware of what is going on. For Sophia, the universe is governed by God, a belief that she expresses when she says: 'Thy will be done' (p.257). She follows the rules laid down by religion, which include practising religious rituals such as lighting candles in church and crossing herself, in order to let God resolve any issues that arise, such as her son's tendency to be attracted to other women. Sophia does not act to intervene directly by speaking to Andoni or Barbara; instead, she speaks to the Panagia.

Tradition plays a strong role in the lives of the older characters living in Greek villages. It is interwoven with religion, as in the above example, but it also arises from a style of life that is closely tied to the seasons and to the land. 'Place of Birth' shows cooking and farm routines that are linked to the older people's rural lifestyle. Their understanding of how the world works is informed by tradition and superstition, such as Sophia's belief that a baby died because the pregnant mother ate bananas (p.359). Sophia does not challenge these beliefs; they guide her and provide her with a response to things that happen in the world.

## The search for meaning & fulfilment

Many of Farmer's stories explore an individual's journey towards self-knowledge and fulfilment. Farmer often presents this journey as a spiritual one. We are introduced to characters who are searching for meaning in experiences they have and to better understand their place in the world.

Farmer presents the quest for personal fulfilment as a difficult yet necessary pursuit, especially for her female characters. For some of these characters, personal fulfilment comes before duty towards family and loved ones. While we may judge their actions as selfish and damaging to the family unit, the quest for self-fulfilment is overwhelmingly presented as a positive one for women. Farmer's male characters, however, are presented less sympathetically. The philandering husband in 'Caffe Veneto' who returns to seek reconciliation with his wife in 'Matrimonial Home' provides a good example of a character who is guided chiefly by his personal desires, and is oblivious to the pain this causes the women in his life. His behaviour is characterised by a need to follow his own desires and an inability to put his wife's feelings first.

Barbara and Bell are both searching for something more from life than what it has offered them, and both make major decisions in relation to their individual desires or needs: they leave their husbands and children. Farmer provides little information about why this choice is made, although there are hints that the hierarchy of life within a Greek family was in some way restrictive for them.

**Key Point**

Farmer draws a link between the rejection of domestic life and women's personal fulfilment.

In 'Pomegranates', Bell returns to Greece to visit her former mother-in-law. We don't learn the reason for her trip, although it may be to revisit the time when she was still a part of the family and to better understand her reasons for leaving. In 'White Friday' Barbara also appears to be seeking answers to the question of where she truly belongs. She has reached a turning point in her life and, like Bell, revisits her past in order to make sense of her present situation and her future. When the decision is made, it is as if it is made for her and not by her: 'She is going back, it seems. Why? Is this how decisions should be made or make themselves?' (p.312). She appears content not to confront the decision-making process directly, but rather to let it happen at a level of her subconscious mind, and to tell herself that certain signs and omens have affected the outcome. In this respect she is similar to Kyria Sophia, believing in God's will or fate.

In other stories, such as 'A Girl on the Sand' and 'Fire and Flood', a specific event precipitates a character's reassessment of their life. Dimitri, in the former story, is reminded of an event from his youth when a girl's body is washed up on the beach in the present. This memory causes him to reflect on his family's story and the life they have built in Australia since leaving Greece at the end of a war-torn decade. Peter, the protagonist of 'Fire and Flood', is forced to rethink the meaning of his life after a shocking set of events – the tragic and unrelated deaths of the two people closest to him. Peter struggles to find a reason for what has happened. When we encounter him he is adrift, lacking any direction or a base to which he can return. The story conveys a sense of the gradual dissolution of all the things that once gave meaning to Peter's life. As readers, we face these struggles and questions along with the characters and the chance to ask ourselves what we might do in a similar situation.

## Honour

**Key Quote**

> 'A sense of honour: *philotimo*. Or rather, a pride in one's honour ... Perhaps there's no honour free of paradox; no pride either.' (p.344)

Dimitri in 'A Girl on the Sand' talks about honour. It is the only story to tackle this value directly, exploring it in the context of how Dimitri's behaviour affects the honour of his family. The concept is also explored through the pregnant girl, Dimitroula. Dimitri has to work in order to feed his fatherless family and to prevent his sisters from turning to prostitution, which he manages successfully. Dimitroula has been dishonoured by falling pregnant when not married. When Dimitri promises to help her, he keeps his word, enabling her to obtain the abortion that she came for and to return home safely.

Despite Dimitri's exemplary behaviour when young, as a man his whole family is dishonoured when his wife is caught having an affair with a family enemy, and the social stigma is so great that they are forced to emigrate to Australia. Although Dimitri does not dwell on that fact, it is clear that it has shaped his own and his family's destiny, and that the value they place on honour strongly influences their behaviour.

## Home is not a sanctuary

As the title of her second collection of stories *Home Time* (1985) – in which these stories were first published as a set – suggests, Farmer has made the idea of home a key focus of her writing. She does not represent home exclusively as a sanctuary or secure place in which people are nurtured and encouraged to grow; rather, home as it appears in Farmer's stories is also a place in which characters become trapped and from which many seek to escape.

The starkest example of this is the woman in 'A Woman with Black Hair', whose cosy family home is violently invaded and which becomes a site of terror. 'Marina' also shows a character who is slowly driven mad through confinement in her home with her baby, with no support from anyone. In both these stories, home is a trap which also symbolises the psychological or mental trap that both these women become caught in. Marina finds herself in a trap of insanity and crazed helplessness, while the woman rape victim will become trapped by her own fear that the rapist will one day return, a fear that he deliberately instils in her. Both Bell and Barbara also feel trapped by the confines of domesticity, and escape from the limitations of home life as they are presented here.

## Social roles & individuality

Farmer's stories often show the tension that exists between individual identity and social expectations that are often based on a person's gender, particularly in the context of families and family roles. The stories raise questions as to whether the individual should act in their own interests first, or whether the good of the family should take priority.

The Greek family stories in particular show how social expectations clash with the desires of individuals, through the characters of Bell and Barbara. At some point we realise that these two characters have made a choice in favour of their individual autonomy, because in each of the later stories 'Pomegranates' and 'White Friday' we learn that both Bell and Barbara have left their husbands and children. While each character's individual motives for leaving are never explained, events and situations depicted in the stories show us some of the tensions created by social and familial expectations.

## Sexuality

**Key Quote**

"I've understood the other times. I've kept your secrets. Commiserated when it was over. Haven't I? What I *don't* understand is why this time my mother would deserve to be left." (p.194)

Sexuality often functions as a disruptive and destructive element in the stories. It is capable of pulling apart the family unit and, in its worst forms, of being used with violence as a weapon to terrorise and intimidate.

In 'Caffe Veneto', 'Matrimonial Home' and 'Marina', illicit sexual relationships threaten the married couple's unity. Marina fears that her relationship with her husband will end the same way that it began, with him having an affair with another woman, just as he did with her when he was married to Joss. Anne's father leaves her mother to have an affair, causing much pain and uncertainty. These male characters' inability to remain faithful to their partners is the reason for the ensuing difficulties in their relationships, and sexuality is represented as a disturbing element. 'The Harem' also portrays June's sexuality as dangerous or disruptive, causing a rift in the Peterson family. The whole story centres on how men find June attractive and the effect that this has on their behaviour.

The threat posed by female sexuality to the family unit is also portrayed in 'Our Lady of the Beehives', in which father and husband Andoni is attracted to the teenage Voula. In this story, Andoni's feelings for Voula are suddenly altered when his son has an accident, and he retreats into his family unit.

Similarly, 'A Man in the Laundrette' suggests that the mere fact of being a woman can encourage aggressive behaviour in men. The woman writer who is harassed by a young black man is stunned to hear that both the Puerto Rican man and then her boyfriend consider that she is at fault in the matter and that she is somehow responsible for having been picked on. In a more subtle way, 'Home Time' continues this theme of troublesome female sexuality when the woman's writing about the abusive relationships of the older woman in the bar causes her partner to commit the violent gesture of breaking her coffee cup. It is as though her access to a woman's intimate secrets makes her a target for his anger, although as discussed earlier, it may be that he also feels threatened by her talent for and commitment to her writing.

## Motherhood

Key Quote

> 'The baby began its squalling ... She should bath it, but she shrank from its panic, its slithering body dripping soap.' (pp.25–6)

Depictions of motherhood in some of these stories are gritty and confronting, defying the more standard, airbrushed images of mothers who do not question the personal sacrifices they make for the good of their children. Society often punishes women who do not make these sacrifices by labelling them bad mothers. 'Marina' is Farmer's most powerful example of a mother who feels thoroughly alienated by the experience; the horrifying outcome is that she kills her baby.

The paired stories, 'Our Lady of the Beehives' and 'White Friday' as well as 'Place of Birth' and 'Pomegranates', show how both Barbara and Bell leave their families after initially appearing comfortable and at home with them. Both are questioned by older Greek women as to why they left their sons and returned to Australia, but no answers are given. Although these women's stories do not end as tragically as Marina's, they nevertheless challenge many readers' expectations that mothers will always remain with heir children.

## Love offers hope

Alongside the dark themes and ideas running through these stories, Farmer also presents more positive ideas that offer an optimistic way of looking at life. 'Market Day' takes us from Mikri Elpida's initial depressing realisation that she is growing old to her coming to terms with this fact, and her renewed interest in life when she discovers that her niece Nitsa is in love. The cycle of life is represented with both highs and lows from which characters can learn important lessons.

'White Friday' shows a woman who makes a decision about her future based on love and on the hope that her relationship will continue. Barbara returns to Greece after the death of her mother. She is unsure whether to relocate there to be nearer her children or whether to remain in Australia with her lover, despite his non-committal attitude. Barbara ultimately decides to return to him and continue their relationship, even though 'he is lent, not given' (p.312). She is aware she is ageing and of the growing distance between her and her sons. Remembering the warmth of her lover's physical presence seems to be the deciding factor in Barbara's decision, because it is contrasted with the coolness and emotional distance that characterises her relationships with her sons.

# DIFFERENT INTERPRETATIONS

Different interpretations arise from different responses to a text. There is no single correct reading or interpretation of a text. However, an interpretation is more than an 'opinion' – it is the justification of a point of view on the text as a whole, or on one element of it. To present an interpretation of the text based on your point of view you must use a logical argument and relevant evidence from the text to support and strengthen it.

The tension between individual identity and socially dictated roles is a key theme of many of Farmer's stories. The stories exploring families and migration are particularly fruitful for these topics. The following two perspectives show how it is possible to perform different readings of the situations and experiences that these stories foreground.

## Interpretation 1: negative view of family

**Farmer's stories show that family life restricts individuals and destroys relationships.**

Many characters in these stories feel uncomfortable in the roles imposed on them by society. This is especially so in the Greek stories, which show non-Greek individuals struggling to fit into narrow familial roles that have been shaped by tradition and do not allow any flexibility for those who wish to expand or change their roles.

Bell provides the clearest example of a woman who feels trapped by family expectations, as shown in 'Place of Birth' when she wishes to return home to Australia to have her baby and raises the ire of her husband. Note that it is not just the expectations of her husband and Greek family that trap her and make her feel uncomfortable, but also that on another level she is perhaps unconsciously trapped by the needs and wishes of her own parents, who make her feel guilty for not being in Australia. The second story in this pair, 'Pomegranates', shows that Bell subsequently left her husband and child. In some way, family life has proved too restrictive or unsatisfying for her, and she has left the family unit in order to retain her sanity and sense of self.

Similarly, Barbara in 'White Friday' has left Andoni, her husband in 'Our Lady of the Beehives'. His behaviour in this latter story suggests that he is likely to be unfaithful to her; it is possible that it is due to infidelity that Barbara decides to leave him and their sons. Andoni's behaviour, chastising Barbara if ever she flags in her motherhood role, and not allowing her any autonomy or time to herself, could also have contributed to Barbara's need to escape what may have become for her a domestic prison.

Ultimately, relationships in these stories disintegrate and, in extreme cases, the breakdown of individual identity occurs as a result. Marina is an example of a woman who cannot cope with the expectation that her husband and the local Greek women place on her to adjust to motherhood and adapt to its demands. Tragically she loses her mind, her sanity disintegrating in the face of a lack of support and the unceasing demands of her husband and baby. Marina's thoughts remain in her head and she has no-one to share them with. She crumbles because she is unable to give voice to her fears and her worries; she has to repress them and be seen to be coping. However, the pressure is too great. As Marina reflects, 'Dreams will drive me mad' (p.23).

## Interpretation 2: positive view of family

**The stories show that family provides a place for people to flourish.**
The love and support that exist within families and extended family networks enable characters in Farmer's stories to grow and find contentment. Despite experiences of loss and tragedy, the family environment provides support and sustenance to its members.

Even after divorce, the extended networks that characters have built up still provide them with support. Bell's return to her former husband's family in 'Pomegranates' shows the warmth and mutual respect that still exists between the old Greek woman and her former daughter-in-law, as Bell seeks answers to questions about who she is and why her life took the course it did. Her shared past and memories replenish her and provide her with the opportunity to explore her identity by enabling her to compare herself in the present with who she was in the past.

Despite problems with poverty and then dishonour, Dimitri speaks fondly of his family in 'A Girl on the Sand', and it is clear that he has a close relationship with his mother and sisters. His family has lived and remained together through civil war and then migration to a strange land, and they like to reminisce about their past and reflect on their shared experiences.

Mikri Elpida finds solace against the fact of her ageing through her closeness with her niece, Nitsa, and through being part of a large family network in which she is loved and valued. Elpida is able to reflect on her experiences as a young woman by telling Nitsa one of the family stories – the one about how she was blinded. The space of the family provides her with the security of known routines and an assured place in a kinship structure.

# QUESTIONS & ANSWERS

The essay topics below show a range of possible styles and formats, and are suitable for senior English assessment tasks and examinations.

1 'The characters in these stories are powerless to change their fates.'
Discuss.
(Examine the ways in which the author constructs meaning through characters.)

2 How are the characters' lives shaped by the places they live in?
(Demonstrate an understanding of how settings and contexts are linked to characterisation.)

3 'Families in these stories are oppressive structures that stifle individuals.'
Discuss.
(Develop and justify a detailed interpretation of the text.)

4 'Farmer's first-person narrators prevent us from understanding the other characters' points of view.'
Discuss.
(Demonstrate knowledge of how the author uses first-person narration and how it impacts on the reader.)

5 'These stories show the resilience of people in the face of relationship breakdown and change.'
Discuss.
(Consider the ways in which the author constructs meaning through characters and situations.)

6 'Farmer's stories show that home is more than just the place in which we live.'
Discuss.
(Demonstrate your understanding of a key theme and show how the text expresses or implies a point of view and values.)

7 How does the pairing of a number of stories enable us to see the evolution of characters and relationships?
(Consider how the structure of the collection influences our understanding of characters.)

8 'Farmer's stories suggest that people do not always realise the consequences of their actions until it is too late.'
Discuss.
(Develop and justify a detailed interpretation of the text.)

9 'The men in these stories are selfish and individualistic characters who cause women to suffer.'
Discuss.
(Examine the representations of men and how they embody social and cultural values.)

10 'Characters in Farmer's stories find that intercultural relationships cause more problems than they provide benefits.'
Discuss.
(Examine the social and cultural values embodied by the text.)

## Analysing a sample topic

**4. 'Farmer's first-person narrators prevent us from understanding other characters' points of view.' Discuss.**

Begin by thinking about the question and the scope of answer that it requires. This question requires you to understand how narration works, and how our understanding of a text is shaped through the perspective of the person who is telling the story. There are three stories with first-person narrators. Think about who is speaking in each story, and whether they tell just their story, or those of other characters also. Make notes about each story's narrators:

- 'A Woman with Black Hair' – the rapist narrator tries to prevent reader from accessing woman's point of view.
- 'Fire and Flood' – Peter does not try to hide Joan or Marie's points of view; he actively relates them. He conveys information that Joan must have told him, such as what happened during the fire.
- 'A Girl on the Sand' – Dimitri tries to convey Dimitroula's point of view; he recalls dialogue, which lets her speak in her own words.

In a more general sense, this question asks you about how characters' feelings and experiences are conveyed by texts. As a reader, do you gain any idea of how the woman in 'A Woman with Black Hair' experiences the sexual assault and invasion of her home? If so, how is it conveyed, if it is not through a direct speaking voice? What about Joan and Marie in 'Fire and Flood': how do you know what their thoughts and feelings are? These are conveyed partly through direct speech (the words enclosed in quotation marks), and partly through the narrator's descriptions of their behaviour and appearances. The same techniques are used for Dimitroula in 'A Girl on the Sand'.

Look back over the stories. It is clear in 'A Woman with Black Hair' that the main dynamic between the narrator and the woman is that of observer and observed, of predator and victim. The use of 'I' and 'she' sets up this dynamic. The narrator gives us plenty of information about his thoughts and experiences. Through his observations of the woman's behaviour and reactions we learn what she may be going through: from her annoyance at finding one of her roses in the kitchen, to her terrified face when she realises that he is in her room. This means that much of our understanding is mediated or relayed through the narrator.

How does this impact on our understanding of the woman's experience? This is what you have to consider and discuss in your response. Are there other ways that we can access her experience? We can also develop an understanding of what she is experiencing through empathy, and through our knowledge of depictions of sexual violence towards women in other literary and film texts. The statement carries an assumption that we cannot access someone else's experience unless they describe it to us directly. However, as discussed, there are other ways of understanding what a person is going through. Ask yourself the same questions about the other two stories. They are different in that the narrators are not seeking to withhold information about the other characters; in fact, they try to show readers what those characters have suffered. Both Peter and Dimitri are sympathetic witnesses to other people's pain; Peter is more intimately involved in their pain as he too suffers loss.

As the question is asking you to respond to a statement, you need to form a clear contention or opinion. Use the information that you have generated by working through the above issues to decide on a stance.

### Sample introduction

Here is one way of approaching the topic, outlined in a sample introduction:

> The narrators in 'A Woman with Black Hair', 'Fire and Flood' and 'A Girl on the Sand' vary in their accounts of other characters' thoughts and feelings. Whereas the rapist narrator in 'A Woman with Black Hair' seeks to control not only his victim's words and actions, but also the reader's response, Peter and Dimitri try to convey the suffering of the people with whom they are involved. The first-person narrative voice can be used to restrict the reader's understanding, but it can also provide powerful insights into the experiences of other characters.

### Explore relationships

With this topic you will need to explore the narrators' relationships to other characters. It is important to consider how in 'A Woman with Black Hair' the victim is only allowed to speak according to a script prepared by the rapist, and how she is always referred to in the third person as 'she', reinforcing her status as an object and denying her an opportunity to speak with her own voice. However, although we as readers cannot access her feelings and thoughts directly, as we can with the rapist's, nor as easily as we can those of the characters in the two other stories, our observations of her fear, coupled with our empathy for her as a fellow human being who is being made to suffer, enable us to identify with her experience.

The rest of your response should show which elements of the stories give insight into what the characters are feeling. Examine whether the narrators' attitudes towards them change, and look at the balance between narrators' points of view and those of characters who are not narrating.

### Conclusion

Ensure that your conclusion reiterates points made in the essay and that it reaffirms your position on the issue. You should emphasise how narrative point of view does not solely determine how we respond to a text.

## SAMPLE ANSWER

**6. 'Farmer's stories show that home is more than just the place in which we live.' Discuss.**

Home is more than a physical space: it is a concept that means different things to different people. Farmer's stories show how an understanding of home is linked to migration, family and identity for a number of characters, and how their relationships to 'home' shape their experiences. For some, being far from their home makes them vulnerable, while for others, home is turned from a sanctuary to a site of terror. No two characters experience home in quite the same way.

It is telling in 'Place of Birth' when Bell says that she wishes to have her baby at home, that Kyria Sophia understands that she wants a home birth. 'Why not? I had all mine here'. Bell, however, means that she wants to return to Australia from Greece, which would entail taking her husband with her and taking the baby away from her Greek in-laws. For Sophia, home refers to her Greek home, the one where her family was born and raised. In Greek family structure, Bell has been absorbed into her husband's family, and no-one considers that she is referring to her own Australian family and place of birth. The title refers to both the place of birth of the baby, which is the underlying focus of the story, and also to Bell's place of birth, which is exerting a pull on her at his time in her life. Bell needs to explain to her husband and in-laws not only which home she really means, but also why she wants to return there, because for them it is bizarre that she wants to go away from her Greek family.

Home can also symbolise a union between people, such as in 'Matrimonial Home'. Matthew returns to see Margaret after having instructed the solicitor not to proceed with selling the family home, an act which precedes and prefigures his attempt to reconcile with his wife after having left her for a younger woman. His ease in the house and the way in which both he and Margaret quickly resume old, established routines such as coffee in bed, symbolises the strength of their relationship and its support through old habits which are hard to break. It is clear that this relationship is not yet over and may never be.

A character's distance from familiar territory can make them feel destabilised and in need of another kind of home where they can feel secure. The woman writer in 'A Man in the Laundrette' and 'Home Time' is living with a man with whom she is no longer in love, and who openly demonstrates hostility towards her. When she encounters an unfriendly stranger (the man in the launderette), she is left with only her writing to comfort her. For this woman, writing provides a form of 'home' in its familiar activity and provision of a space in which she can explore events and make sense of them, in a way that is impossible with her boyfriend. Significantly, the title 'Home Time' expresses her realisation that it is time for her to leave her partner and the US and return to Australia.

Although home may represent a sanctuary to many people, it is such a potent symbol that its meaning may be reversed so that what was home becomes a prison. Marina's postnatal depression and lack of support mean that her home becomes the place where she loses her mind and commits the terrible act of murdering her newborn baby. The woman with black hair, who clearly has created a cosy and loving home for herself and her children, finds that it has become a place of terror when its sanctity is violated by a cruel and sadistic rapist intent on turning her into a prisoner of her own fear. For these women, their homes will never be the same again after these experiences.

A home may be located in a physical space but it is often much more than that. A home is a place with cultural and historical significance, which often has an intensely personal meaning. It can also be an intangible thing, such as the practice of writing, which feels familiar and reminds a person of who she is in the world, or a sense of a place as safe and inviolable.

# REFERENCES & READING

## Text

Farmer, Beverley 1996, *Collected Stories*, University of Queensland Press, St Lucia.

## References

Clancy, Laurie 2007, *Beverley Farmer Biography*, http://biography.jrank.org/pages/4306/Farmer-Beverley.html

Jacobs, Lyn 2001, *Against the Grain: Beverley Farmer's Writing*, University of Queensland Press, St Lucia.

Murdoch, Anna King 1994, 'The Power of One Greek Woman', *The Age*, 28 February, p.9.

## Other titles in this series

*A Lesson Before Dying*
*A Man for All Seasons*
*A View from the Bridge*
*Angela's Ashes*
*The Baghdad Blog*
*Blade Runner*
*Blueprints for a Barbed-Wire Canoe*
*Border Crossing*
*Breaker Morant*
*Brilliant Lies*
*Cabaret*
*Citizen Kane*
*Dead Letter Office*
*Diving for Pearls*
*Don't Start Me Talking Lyrics 1984–2004*
*Dream Stuff*
*Falling*
*Fine Line*
*First They Killed My Father*
*Fly Away Peter*
*Gattaca*
*Generals Die in Bed*
*Girl with a Pearl Earring*
*Going Home*
*Hamlet*
*Hard Times*
*Henry Lawson's Short Stories*
*Home*
*I for Isobel*
*If This is a Man*
*I'm Not Scared*
*Inheritance*
*In the Lake of the Woods*
*Jackson's Track*
*Lantana*
*Life of Galileo*
*Look Both Ways*
*Maestro*
*Macbeth*
*Medea*
*Minimum of Two*
*Montana 1948*
*Night*
*Nineteen Eighty-Four*
*No Great Mischief*
*Oedipus the King*
*Of Love and Shadows*
*One True Thing*
*Only the Heart*
*Othello*
*Romulus, My Father*
*Selected Poems (Sylvia Plath)*
*Shakespeare in Love*
*Stolen*
*Sky Burial*
*Tess of the D'Urbervilles*
*The Accidental Tourist*
*The Age of Innocence*
*The Chant of Jimmie Blacksmith*
*The Curious Incident of the Dog in the Night-time*

continues overleaf

*The Divine Wind*
*The Freedom of the City*
*The Great Gatsby*
*The Hunter*
*The Kite Runner*
*The Longest Memory*
*The Outsider*
*The Penguin Book of First World War Poetry*
*The Plague*
*The Player*
*The Quiet American*
*The Stories of Tobias Wolff*
*The Things They Carried*
*The Third Man*
*The Wife of Martin Guerre*
*The Year of Living Dangerously*
*Things Fall Apart*
*Triage*
*What's Eating Gilbert Grape?*